I0438247

The Jr.'s Guide To Hunting

Hayden C. Kennedy

Hayden Kennedy

The Jr.'s Guide to Hunting
Volume 1

Copyright © 2014 by Hayden C. Kennedy

All Rights Reserved. Printed in the United States of America. No part of this book may be used or reproduced in any manner whatsoever without the written permission of the author.

Book design and type formatting by Hayden Kennedy.

All rights reserved.

ISBN:150014875X
ISBN-13:9781500148751

Hayden Kennedy

DEDICATION

To my family, friends, and my little dog—Oliver.

Hayden Kennedy

CONTENTS

Hayden Kennedy

ACKNOWLEDGMENTS

First of all, I'd like to thank my dad, Jeff
Kennedy. He helped me a lot and taught me
how to write books.
I'd like to thank my hunter safety teachers
who taught me a lot about hunting. I'd also
like to thank my uncle Kevin Neubauer who
gave me my first gun and showed me how to
shoot. Thanks to my grandpa, Loren
Neubauer for inspiring me to want to become
a great outdoorsmen. Thanks to uncle Clyde
for being an expert at killing stuff.

Hayden Kennedy

PART I

SAFETY FOR KID HUNTERS

1

GUN SAFETY

Gun safety is very important! First, you always want to open the action during hunting. An action is the part that cocks the shell or bullet into the chamber (pump action shotgun has a pump as the action). Or if you have a pump action gun you'll want to leave it un-cocked.

A guns butt (the back of the gun) should always be pressed tightly against your shoulder. That way it will not fly out of your arms. Every time you hold a rifle/shotgun you should always hold it with both hands. NEVER, ever point the muzzle at something you are not going to shoot.

This is especially true of people and water. Bullets or shotgun shot might bounce off and hit something you don't want it to hit.

Never shoot ammo straight up in the sky because it will fall back down and might hit you or something else causing serious injury.

Hayden Kennedy

4

2

PHYSICAL SAFETY

During long hunts you should drink plenty of water. If you get injured during your hunt, tell your hunting partner that you need to sit out for as long as is necessary.

Do not climb with your gun because it is very dangerous. Climbing with your gun could result in really bad injuries or even dying.

If you happen to get hypothermia tell your

hunting partner to get help. It is very important to have a hunting partner during any hunt because you can get severely injured while hiking and stalking your prey.

If you do not have a partner to go with, then either cancel your trip or find someone else who can go with you. I would recommend bringing a couple snacks just in case. If you get lost, at least you'll have some rations to feed you while you're waiting to be rescued.

In fact, I recommend that you bring beverages such as water or other drinks that will keep you hydrated.

Safety tip: Wear orange so other hunters in

the area don't mistake you as game. Always remember: colorblind animals won't know you're wearing orange, but other hunters can see the orange from a long distance (unless they also are colorblind which would be very unfortunate).

Hayden Kennedy

3

ANIMAL SAFETY

You should respect animals around you such as chipmunks and squirrels. Squirrels are not even legal to hunt in small game season in Idaho anyway. Check your local state laws for rules that you should abide by.

You should not destroy animals' homes on purpose. Instead, you should help them by cleaning the environment around you. You should pick up your shells that you shot. If you don't that is fine.

And do not litter whatsoever because animals might move out because of all the trash.

Plus, even if you see trash you should pick it up. Animals that you don't hunt should be respected as well as you treat a pet or someone else's pet.

If you don't know if you are allowed to shoot an animal just ask your hunting partner or wait for them to tell you to shoot it. It is legal if you find a different animal you are not hunting you are welcome to shoot it if it is legal. But if it is not legal, then don't shoot it.

Always make sure you know the safety rules

for animals in your area or state first.

Hayden Kennedy

PART II
PROPER EQUIPMENT

Hayden Kennedy

4

KNIVES

Knives are the first tools on the list. Knives are very important. They help gut and skin the animal you shot.

If you and your hunting partner don't have any knives, then tell him/her to get one or figure something out (try your local hunting story if necessary). A knife will help you to cut something such as rope or rubber. Picking the right knife is very important. Some knives have different jobs.

For instance, a boning knife can't do a kitchen knives' job. Keep it cased or closed so it doesn't cut you or any clothing.

Do not play with knives such as twirling or pretending to kill something. Blades are very sharp. I myself was cut by a knife in the finger as a little kid and I can tell you getting cut really hurts. So do not play with knives at all. Only use them for hunting purposes.

If you happen to get cut, squeeze you're hand and put pressure on the wound and tell an adult. In fact, you shouldn't even handle the knife without permission. You should carry a handkerchief just in case. Make sure you know how to tie a knot in case you need to make a makeshift tourniquet.

In addition to gutting and skinning an animal, knives can also be very useful tools for other things such as cutting string, opening cans of food, and sharpening sticks (and don't play with sharp sticks either).

Hayden Kennedy

5

GUNS

Guns are the most important tools for small game.

But rifles are too harsh for small game. The best gun for small game is a shotgun from .410-.16 gauge. That's what I used to kill a wild rabbit. Then I used my knife to gut, and skin the rabbit.

Slugs are for shotguns and are better for

hunting deer (by "slugs" I don't mean those little slimy creatures you find in your backyard). Slugs are basically bullets for shotgun shells. But, if you live in the east, you may not be allowed to use them. Again, check your local laws so you know the rules.

Rifles are best for big game such as deer, elk, moose, etc. You need the right kind of gun for the right kind of animal.

For instance, a .28 gauge is better for a rabbit than .10 gauge shotgun. In fact, a .10 gauge shotgun is the most powerful shotgun and will literally blow your rabbit to bits.

Pistols are used for big game such as bear. Some pellet rifles are used for hunting small game. .22 rifles are not allowed too hunt big

game. But you can hunt certain small game

with them.

Hayden Kennedy

6

CLOTHING

Proper clothing is needed for any type of hunt. On warm hunts you should wear cool clothing. For cold hunts you should wear warm clothing like sweatshirts or coats.

And hats are essential. That is because you lose most body heat through your head and ticks can fall on your head. Cammo clothing is important so animals do not see you coming. I prefer cammo hats as well.

Also, you might see some people wear some orange, especially their hats. DO NOT dress as game like deer hats if its deer season, or raccoon hats for small game season. That can get you killed.

Orange clothes help so other people can see you and don't shoot you. I myself occasionally wear orange. But only my hat because I don't have any hunting clothes besides cammo.

Hayden Kennedy

7

THE BARREL

The barrel of the gun is the long metal piece sticking out the front of the gun. It helps and determines the range of the bullet trajectory.

The barrel will usually have the caliber or gauge of the gun. The longer the barrel the quieter it is.

The barrel could be damaged so treat it

with GREAT respect. And a damaged barrel can be serious and cause severe damage or even death.

Some guns have different sized barrels. That usually happens according to the size of the gun. Even some tiny pistols don't even have barrels! While some rifles can have very long ones. Do not hit someone on the head with the barrel of a gun. It could cause severe injury. And, your hunting trip will be ruined.

Always and only point the barrel in the direction you want to shoot. Never point the barrel of a gun at anything you don't intend to shoot and kill (this means don't point it at people or other animals you aren't allowed to shoot).

Hayden Kennedy

8

THE STOCK

The stock is the long wooden part that you press your shoulder on to keep the gun tight. With some guns you can remove the stock and replace it with a bigger one when you grow bigger.

Sometimes there is a black plastic or rubber part on the back of the stock. This part is called the butt. The butt is the very back of the gun that you press tightly against your shoulder.

NOTE: do not shoot a gun more powerful than you can handle. It is possible that it may blast out of your arms and crack the stock. That happened to my dad when he was a kid and shot a gun too big for him.

Remember: the stock is very hard so don't hit anyone, it could cause severe injury.

Hayden Kennedy

9

THE ACTION

The action is the part of a gun that loads the bullet/shot in the chamber.

Various actions can be very different from each other. For example, the bolt action and the lever action are two different kinds of loading mechanisms.

In some cases, some actions don't load bullets into the chamber. Like lever action, which pops the shell. But pump actions pop out shells and load a bullet/shot into the chamber.

If you know where they are and know how to use them, then you can soon become great hunter.

Tip: Make sure you know exactly how to use all the parts of your gun before you go out hunting. This will make your experience much better and you'll stay very safe.

Hayden Kennedy

10

THE MUZZLE

The muzzle of a rifle and a shotgun are very different.

For instance, the rifle's barrel is grooved so the bullet will spin when shot. But the shotgun barrel is smooth so all the pellets can slide through the barrel. If you accidentally fall and hit the barrel of a gun on the ground, make sure there is no dirt or grass in there, or else when shot it has a high risk of blowing up.

NOTE: do not look straight down the barrel to make sure there is nothing stuck down there, just ask an adult to do it. Never hit the barrel on a tree or log. It is extremely dangerous and stupid.

EPILOGUE

EXTRA HUNTING ADVICE FROM HAYDEN

If you are driving in a truck while hunting, if you are by the door put the gun on the opposite side of the door. The reason why I said that was because I had made a big mistake doing it. Here's what happened: my uncle, my cousin, and I were out hunting for grouse. My cousin spotted a well-hidden grouse in the in the brush. They were going to let me take the first shot at it. So I excitedly hopped out the truck, but I accidentally hit the muzzle of the gun on the dirt. The grouse seemed to notice me falling out of the truck, so it flew away. I am still haunted to this day about that grouse hunt. But I am at least proud the next time I went hunting I scored by killing a rabbit the first time I shot it. (I have a picture of the rabbit).

Do not throw or toss a gun around. The gun could break or even worse shoot off. (Possibly hitting you).

If you are using a scope, you can steady it more by holding your breath. This helps by calming yourself down and slowing your heart rate.

Keep your action open when not sighting on prey. Because you can accidentally pull the trigger and hitting you/hunting partner or scaring game.

ABOUT THE AUTHOR

Hayden Kennedy is an avid kid hunter and loves all things about the outdoors and the sport of hunting.

Hayden Kennedy

www.ingramcontent.com/pod-product-compliance
Lightning Source LLC
Chambersburg PA
CBHW050521290526
45786CB00007B/2648